T0063021

A SEASON OF TENDERNESS AND DREAD
a collection of poems, photographs and meditations

abu bakr solomons

*For my teachers; Hilary Tembe, Robbie Green, Raymond Leitch
& Morgan Macarthur-Merrington who taught me the power of words-
and all those who walked this path with me.*

Camerado, this is no book
Who touches this touches a man
(Is it night? Are we here together alone?)
It is I you hold and who holds you.
I spring from the pages into your arms –
decease calls me forth.

WALT WHITMAN: Leaves of Grass

Published by Botsotso in 2016

Box 30952
Braamfontein
2017
South Africa

email: botsotso@artslink.co.za
website: www. botsotso.org.za

ISBN 978-0-9814205-9-2

Cover and text make-up:
Vivienne Preston

Contents

1.

Small adventure

Quite arbitrarily someone christened Mondays
a day to do weekend washing;
a declaration that assaulted
the sanctity of an azure sky,
the crispness of a simple morning.

Without any prompting,
one rebels against such ruthless tyranny,
pursues the possibility of a small adventure –
even in a supermarket –
merely to obliterate the pedestrian;
nothing epic – just a single epiphany
to endanger the orthodoxy
of such deadly decrees.

It arrives. At the entrance,
an Indonesian angel rolling paper-thin pastry,
her supple hands dipped in peanut oil.
She folds dollops of feta into fresh spinach leaves
then phyllo-sheaths;
rolls popped astutely into sizzling oil –
lifted with meticulous timing,
brown, flawless.
A latent vow to scoff at spring rolls vanishes
instantaneously.

'From Indonesia?' 'Yes. Java.'
'Want to go there soon.'
'Insha'Allah. Yes.
Sheik Yusuf. Macassar.
Kramat. June. Very hot.'
'Tsunamis? Ha ha.'
'No. Insha'Allah.'

Her voice, a sweet promise
of safety for the wings of desire –

sailing round a thousand islands,
listening to familiar incantation

tracing perfumed paths of saints –
Insha'Allah!

2.

Ageing

There is a community of folk,
often invisible, overlooked
somewhat during busy days.

They move slowly, with ease,
making time seem insignificant
yet the morning's pre-eminent.

Neat, meticulous, hair groomed,
their style's perfunctory,
carefully weather-conditioned.

Sometimes there's a hint of glamour:
an emphasized eyebrow, ruby lips,
blue-rinsed hair, spiffy cap.

Shopping is sound and sensible,
an odd small indulgence tossed in,
hesitantly.

There are signs that ankles hurt,
a nerve pinches, an eyelid sags,
copper bangles are a panacea.

Going home is about settling into orderliness,
where waiting is routine.
Memory is a visitor.

Peace is paleness, a soft skin,
cup of tea and a light muffin,
stroking a cat in a scanty room

where the air is fresh,
light dim.

3.

Death's not about dying anymore

Death is not about dying anymore:
about dismembered bodies,
putrid carcasses stacked
on mortuary shelves or blood-soaked pavements;
or the wailing of fractured infants in the arms
of surrogate mothers;
or fathers seeking children,
mothers burying husbands,
shroudless in nameless trenches.

In the midst of life is a kind of death
that blames and bribes and finds
countless ways to feed the lunacy:
it's about not being able to resist unequivocally,
to put your foot into it,
feel the weight of the world behind it;
it's about not finding one's voice,
a language not flirting with deceit,
conviction not suffering cowardice.

Death is humanity commiserating
in the heart of a conflagration,
tyrannous times lamenting with fake tears;
puerile and babbling fervently.

Death is not about dying anymore;
it's about waiting and seeing
the pathos and absurdity of it.

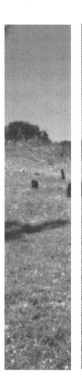

4.

Love, mined

Love that is buried in a memory can be mined,
unearthed, brought to the surface,
raised towards the light,
and there be duly resurrected,
stroked, brushed, restored in shafts of the heart;
strung together ruby red,
glowing ceaselessly in eras
when mad men, mayhem, anarchic adventures,
hatred and greed,
shun love.

Between sediments of time,
love's cooled with tender songs, loyalty sublime,
yet stays undefiled,
intact and alive.

To revive such a love is to rebuke shadows,
defy age, the tyranny of time, foolish frailty;
love buried in memory is a rare find
yet a gift tied to time: sobering sorrows,
sombre days.

5.

Shells

Within the watery swirls of speckled contours,
sealed in cold comfort,
a hollowed creation fills
as rippling tides flow over a hard cone
into crevices that once housed a nascent kernel,
curled and concealed.

Now, too, bone-dry words,
shells of meanings,
hang above the lifeless beach –
an aftermath of loss.
The domed sky's bereft;
two silent gulls stare
at the still, turgid ocean.

6.

You and I

You, I,
we turned them
into gods and goods:

Adam
Krishna
Buddha
Abraham
Jesus
Moses
Muhammad
(May there be peace upon them)

You and I, our fragile selves
blinded by self-seeking hungers,
goaded by insatiable yearnings
for worldly things.

They came to declare the Supreme Being –
infinitude,
in the midst of our feverish ploys
to grasp the everlasting.

They arrived as servants of their Lord;
to seek, obey, declare the Oneness,
illuminate a Path for us to follow
with pure hearts.

Instead, we melted them into golden calves,
belligerent idols of our egos,
blasting the unity of intelligent life
into millions of cosmic fragments.

They came to warn us of that fatal tendency,
speaking His name in words that history transcribed . . .
worked tirelessly, predicting our desires, unbridled,
would burst into flames of fury, conflagration . . .

They guided us to invoke the Unseen mindfully
with simple beads & chants proclaiming love . . .

and so defy the captains of industry's veneration of matter,
and reclaim the brilliance of Unity.

Cave

It's believed a cave's a heart-core;
hollowness into which to ascend,
swirl in its vortex, allow the light
to illuminate a vision from within.

There, darkness is a different blindness,
blurring lines, walls;
a veil to be lifted in the hour.

In the cave, signs from everywhere exist
only in the heart, interpreting.

Sublime fever, an intoxication
severing ties with all but Love,
and then two sounds, a word:

Re-ad.

It signals the descent to rocks, trees,
a touch of a faded tunic, dust on sandals.
Dishevelled hair, sun rising on the edge,
the forlorn date palms sway with the wind:
Welcome. Welcome. Welcome.

The fever subsides, day dawns.
World, listen to the wars of words;
the old is displaced by the ancient.
First there's disquiet, later, peace.

8.

These days

These days we measure progress by the extent
to which anguished cries
can be kept at bay –

how long these can be contained,
prevented from exploding
onto the pavements, into the streets,
creating uncomfortable chaos.

Development is still about constructing
clever nomenclatures
that will put things
into proper perspective.

We have, in a considerably brief period
evolved remarkable ways
of defining 'political correctness'-
it's about dressing appropriately in parliament,
flamboyantly ,
not identifying with the poor overtly.

Nowadays, we define indignation etc.
as 'not being able to perceive the value
of the compromises that were made ... '
of not speculating enough about
'What could have happened if ... '

Let's face it, man:
it takes a group of well-groomed,
well-oiled, well-fed, well-heeled
previously disadvantaged gentlemen
to assess all these
beguiling contradictions.

The rest of us are just doomed to remain
dumb, damned irrelevant, irreverent,
irredeemably ungrateful
for the little that we know,
and the little that we have.

9.

Palsied Paradigm

On the surface, the explanations and justifi-
cation seem
acutely rational & in accordance with sound
principles.

Each action sufficiently substantiated with
evidence –
historical and current – there can be little
room for any doubt.

Further endorsement and ratification's
brought into the domain
of the Divine: love, cosmic obedience &
relevance.

Yet there's often a question dangling, left to
be answered:
who is ultimately the real benefactor in this
exchange?

He? She? Us? Them?
All of us? Some?

Why is there a furtive inevitability, predicta-
bility, in such scenarios
as to who teaches, listens, loses, gains?

Finally, not conclusively, why is it that the
victor, one who gains most,

10.

Change

Down here, in the south, seasons are not changing anymore:
not even the hues of the leaves proclaim it in the suburbs.

Transitions are transfixed in a bubble;
words that flow from dead mouths, contrite cartoons on the daily news.

Promises are paper trails written, revised, without authenticity;
shredded, filling waste-paper bins.

Change's a word that has mutated into the heads
of a foreign-tongued monster rebuking any interrogation.

Even the air seems petrified, days warm but windless,
an atrocity in the townships obstructing a view.

The struggle is to rise above rates of inflation,
scrape, mingy on minor luxuries then dutifully ending days.

Tarnished medallions are generously awarded to obsequious followers
seeking to fill coffers of commissars.

Life's not listening to the symphony of solidarity any longer
but about humming (sad) songs in lonely lanes.

11.

Mid-morning

Mid-mornings's crisp and subdued,
dark clouds, expectant, covet the sky,
imminent storm's restrained.

A tall pine tree stands clean and erect,
branches weave the chilly chasms between earth and sky.

The spare light has pared excess to quintessentials,
present signs of the day remain imperceptible.

Some wary workers amble round
dallying for the day's deliverance.
A vendor re-arranges some bags.

Sitting cross-legged, a busker on a pavement
hums an old tune.
In a frosty window a newsfeed
obtrudes a reverie in a serene season:
the world scoffs simple things,
the symmetry of silence.

Don't let the sun catch you cryin'
so yesterday's minstrel croons.

12.

Moedertaal	Mother tongue
Ek woon in jou gebroke woorde	I live in your broken words
nie in Stellenbosch se *manors* nie	not in the manor houses of Stellenbosch
maar in ou huise en stories van *Bokaap;*	but in the old houses and stories of the BoKaap
in daai strate soos	in those streets like
Langmark	Longmarket
Chiappini	Chiappini
Roos	Rose
Pentz	Pentz
Daar waar ou *Tuans,* eerste leerkragte,	There where old Tuans*, first teachers
hulle Godsdienstige lesse voltooi,	completed their Godfearing lessons
en *surahs* geskryf het.	and wrote their *surahs*
Ek woon saam met jou op boere se plase	I live with you on the farms of Afrikaners
waar sterk, swart slawe geslaan was	where strong black slaves were beaten
by base met Bybel en sjambok,	by bosses with the Bible and sjamboks
daai verlore ouens	those lost fellows
wat na alles gestrewe het	who strived for
wat die wereld vir hulle opoffer	everything that the world had to offer.

<table>
<tr><td>

in die nuwe 'dispensation'.
'dispensation'.

Ek huil saam met jou, oor die belaglikheid
absurdity

die malheid
staan saam met jou
want jy leef, nog steeds,
in my ouers se woorde:

Basta! Bristin! Blatjang!
Kaparangs.Tamaletjies!

Bagaartes.

Toe hulle verlief raak, mekaar ontmoet
in love
in die koue winter van ons land,
land
rond gestap het op die *pier*
around on the *pier*
(nou die *Heerengracht* genoem),
Heerengracht),

toe gebruik hulle vir jou
om mekaar te leer ken –
Die Skepper het geglimlag,

en toe bestaan ek.

</td><td>

in the new

I cried with you over the

the madness
stood by you
because you are still alive
in the words of my parents:

Basta! Bristin! Blatjang!

Kaparangs.Tamaletjies!
Bagaartes.

When they met and fell

in the cold winter of our

ambled

(now called the

they used you
to learn to know each other
The Creator then smiled,

forged me into existence.

</td></tr>
</table>

Seeing, fundamentally

A blanket of fresh, green grass joins
   the edge of a luminous lake;
its placid surface like a sheet of glass
   to a row of hazy, grey mountains that touch the sky,
seeping into a silvery, winter dome –

Soft lines at the edges blur and join
   earth, mountain and sky
so beauty's consummate, an unbroken 'scape
   sealed quietly for the eyes.
Like truth, this fullness cannot fade.
   But coherence is soon dissolved
by the curious mind into its parts:

<pre>
          Grass
Lake   Mountains
      Clouds   Sky
</pre>

So observing fundamentals emphasizes distinction
   but chains each to its own nature.
Imprisoned by the eyes
   Oneness then fades,
slowly splintering into fragments:

The whole sacrificed for the parts
   which may coalesce
      unifying again.

Heart-harvest

There's a season when nightfall is early to gather sweet sorrow,
scattered seedlings of summer.

Before falls of snowstorms, darker days with torrential rains
flush flotsam of love's wreckage.

Here we are walking into Spring with light showers and early sounds,
flowering memory in morningrise.

Vast fields awaken with a hint of radiance that kindles yesterdays' buds
snug under a melting frost.

Battering gales are so tempered as cool winds waft between winter
and phantoms' dance under trees.

So wintry spells are eclipsed as sunshine slips, peccadillos nurse an ache from
heart-harvesting: free lyrics; lilting, songs everlasting.

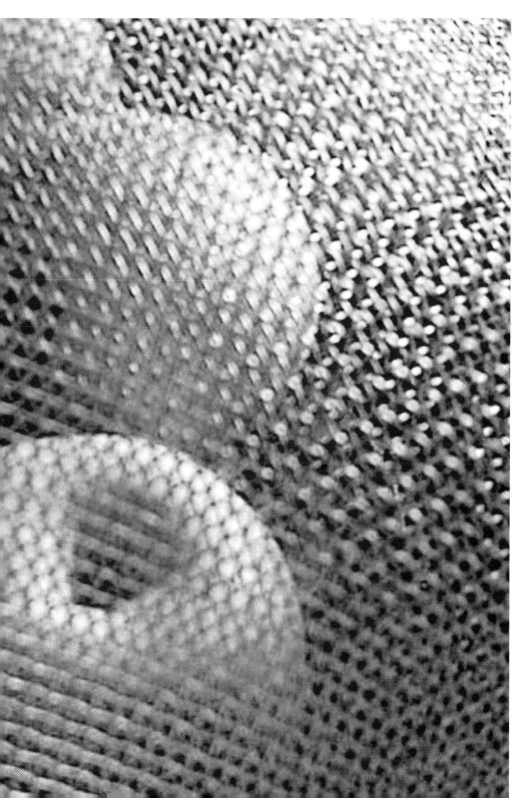

Salvation

Salvation's seeking through a tunnel engulfed in darkness;
its walls encrusted with empty shells
damp with brittle bits of spent life glistening sadly.

At the edge, waves break on silvery sands,
a stream of pale whiteness, blue haze of the sky:
signs of accord between body and lost soul.

But the end's a mirage, an oasis where water and air
transmute into mist. You stretch your hands to hold
beauty that escapes grasp.

Ultimately, salvation's not smooth touchdown,
a place, as some have simply said,
but a new vision – impetus to charter a novel course.

16.

Meditation on Tranquillity

Tranquillity is transient, disrupted by memory, a need –
yours, someone else's;
rattling in the gut in the middle of the night,
a noise, wanting to be heard and appeased . . .

. . . it is short-lived, like a piece of a dream, that feels pleasant,
but disappears
without cautioning or signaling alarm bells;
it slides away, escapes before grasping its allure.

It could return though like an un-announced guest, in a moment
when you least expect its appearance, but fearing it will soon vanish makes you
cautious, almost aloof

... so that when, predictably, it exits after a war has abated, its loss
is not mourned, instead what remains is a yearning
for its swift return .

inheriting, indignation

you, who dream during my waking hours, mundane routines, conjure
visions when stars sigh in frost-bitten skies, drawing closure with
word-gifts, winnowed through cyberspace; you who groom, colour your hair
in chic salons, defying unyielding time, snip dried sunflower stalks of a
past, pious summer, plant doomed pink & blue hydrangeas in yuletide,
northern storms, blooms that bask triumphant, sundrenched in the Cape.

your sedate soirees surreptitiously muffle moans of aborigines, even the
sea's symphony mimics war cries of seared souls, debarred from the
pantheon and sweeping coniferous landscapes to make room for pale
natives, querulous flotsam from Africa.

i cease sparring with bungling bureaucrats on dour missions for change,
at sunset your freshly-baked meat pies resuscitate the dull day.

there and here, in between, a thousand yesterdays threaten to disappear;
in our lifeboat we salvage dalliances of restive youth, with nets too weak
to hold , shards of broken promises become tableaux of tentative
tomorrows, daring to arrive, pages recording tender liaisons threaten to
be exhumed from a deep bold bosom of blue-grey *Hoeri-Kwagga,**
ethereal in the Bokaap.

those are times when geography fails to dismember, when songs do not
appease hearts, then distance between worlds, eras, remains a stubborn
separation.

•   *Hoeri-Kwagga*   Early khoisan name for Table Mountain
       ('mountain by the sea')

18.

Memoirs

Forget memoirs -
let the life-blood of our stories trickle through hearts,
weave itself into daily exchanges,
be revived in simple repertoires
of busy days and sunset chatter;
let no one desecrate what was lovely and lyrical,
falsify with pompous grandeur and ceremony.

Power dictates history, corrupts narratives.
Memoirs may be cooked, crafted, perhaps contrived,
tailor-made to stroke egos, sanctify medals
and baptize blunders;

In the heart, deceit's a dirty word.

There lies raw history's unalloyed sequences;
blinding lies, that concealed, seemed benign –
let memory there expire piously.
It will be a more dignified demise,
untarnished by obsequious obituary.

Erasure

I drew a part of my life
you were in it

Winnowed it to you with tender hands, real, authentic
blooming in fields of sunshine –
a thousand hearts breathed life into its life

I gave it allegiance in a land where loyalty
is anathema, incarcerated

Memory overflowed with narratives of golden eras
celebrated in irrepressible sunrise

Yet foreign tongues, old generals
archived our aphorisms in hovels of neglect

Your forgetting conveniently, too, a placebo
threadbare trick of thieves –

Turning fields of fecund seasons into dark plains of lies

Crossing with Crocodiles

(in memory of the late Comrade Dullah Omar)
An old comrade once warned at the height of the revolution:
Negotiating with the enemy would be like trying to cross the river
on the back of a crocodile ...

The river is a place of darkness and contradictions

(who was he referring to at the time
        when he uttered those words?)

Perhaps it was clear then; the line between the enemy and the victims
(crocodiles and those who wished to cross):
those on the right and others perched on the left,
they knew the crocodile and recognized treacherous waters:

For the river is a place of darkness, of contradictions.

Twenty years later the waters turned murky;
the old comrade has died and his wisdom's no longer sought,
very few care.

The river is now dark and deeper, swarming with new crocodiles
appearing from somewhere, nowhere, everywhere . . .
(Were they always there, multiplying and waiting?
Hiding somewhere.)

One thing's still certain; it would be dangerous to cross the river
on their backs

For the river remains a place of darkness, contradictions

You can drown in that river or, even worse,
be devoured by ravenous crocodiles that have multiplied.

21.

Forgetting maps

There's a world of snow, bleak and cool,
basking in silence that stills the morning rays

Here, the world awakens, a blue sky seeks pre-eminence
seeping through motley clouds

There, the erudite citizens are burning temples, fraught with fear
hatred and misguidance

Here, the betrayed ravage manicured lawns, spill their anger
into streets, burning the flags of the new democracy

Somewhere, in another corner, another wall's erected,
another war's rehearsed

There's no sign anywhere
of things being the way they're supposed to be

Not even the old maps are useful;
the omnipresence of conflagration declares them obsolete

History's being re-written again
but now in the absence of boundaries

The future is a despot

Freedom is mythologised in the new millennium:
the future of the world will be a despot.

In the early hours while police parley with paperwork
armies of the new republics invade ghettos
to purge marauders & the rancour of resistance;
juggernauts enter as saviours into war-torn dominions
then leave as sinners, perpetrators at the whim
of shrewd generals & their sycophants.

The new emperors' forces, conquistadors of the digital age,
descend upon burning cities raising tattered flags for democracy
(and secure tenders for reconstruction).

Elections are mere ploys rigged by bandits,
dictators who flush ballots & mandates down murky oil pipes
(if the leader's not a stooge);

new regimes whelped by bands of cliques
while nations witness events through HD televisions.
It is an age of the puppet colonies.

> *Men killing each other*
> *For someone else's land*
> *Someone else's dream*

There are never coherent answers for the starving masses.
 'Why is so much being dumped
when we grovel for leftovers in dustbins?'
Elites contrive fake explanations about price controls and margins,
rationalize lack of development.

Slowly, but with certitude,
the marginalised of the world
rise to inhabit the centre
'Occupy Wall Street!'
Their voices, choruses for equity.

In the mines the exploited are shot,
foreign agents flee with their booty,
leave deadly diseases;
well- oiled watchdogs collaborate to kill threats to profit:

> *The wealth of Africa*
> *still siphoned*
> *to colonial masters*

In ancient cities, the disgruntled are bludgeoned with batons,
blatant brutality, dark crusades;
repositories of ancient histories, civilizations,
are reduced to dust:

> *Dust and stones and ruins*
> *not over time but by bombs,*
> *bullies, avarice and horror*

At memorial services for fallen martyrs, someone asks:
'Where are the new cabinet ministers?
They drive in their cars while we mourn
the spilt blood of the heroes.'

Freedom's being idealized, not realized, in the new millennium:
The future is a dangerous despot.

Certitude

Four years of pondering have passed,
remnants of supplications and trials between spirit & body
invent a few lines; still, coherence escapes stubbornly.

Your pages brim with certainty,
deliver recollections that usher in your resurrection smoothly
through jarred lines, careless clichés-
ascension is exclusively for those whose hearts
pay allegiance to the narratives of piety.

You denounce my bag of words,
say they're disingenuous and dismembered.
Your awkward lines are enviable,
ripe with resolution;
usurping my unwritten salutations they leave me
doubtful and melancholic,
bankrupt, vanquished and unholy-
and so certitude vexes enduring reticence.

24.

Rain

Rain's been early, falling from new summer skies;
each cloud wafts with rays of sunshine spreading
quietly across the mowed lawn.

The rough edges of cuts inside heal, mellow,
become smooth, obscured: fervent fears of strife subdue
as tepid raindrops melt mole-heaps.

A comfortable distance follows between numbed incisions
and a change of seasons: safe time's arrived.

Old wounds seem painless, obsolete.
Clarity and clean residues arrive post storms and trials.
Somehow things settle into place
like grace, a holy anaesthesia making sense of uphill;
unexpectedly the pitch of fevered yesterdays' undermined.

There's a gentle spirit ruling now that profundity's curbed,
ease's unrivalled, the heart's allowed to speak.
So a promissory of what lies beyond drizzles,
tacked time forecasts benign showers.

In the garden

   Took the day in my stride and strolled through the verdurous garden
feeding on nascent growth, buds and sounds of earnest doves pecking
at wild seed on moist grass.

   A dalliance with words interrupted, whirled round my head dizzying,
mesmerizing a composed morning, coaxing to be strung into light-lines.
   A vision of the garden drifted to a page of tomorrow,
its charm receding as sight was blurred by a battle of signs and images, mulling
into meaning, digging, tweaking, pausing,
      struggling not to lose the comfort of contemplation,
         the loveliness of lavender blossoms,
and be assured of recapturing in the garden a pious, sweet solitude.

26.

Ah! Nambia

Here in this sprawling, arid landscape,
camelthorn trees, kudu bushes sweeping across sepia slopes,
signs of new eras lie embedded in the sand dunes;
basking in light and shade, perpetually eroding, rising,
the winds are harbingers.

The heat in the heart of the city's interminable seasons are resistant to change;
even when night falls, warm breezes cloy and stifle.
Walking through streets, searching for true signs of a new dispensation,
many names confirm that things have remained intact;
re-arranged with a combo of identities, the old and the new paralleled
as in an incompatible marriage.

You sense a country still dominated by foreigners,
its inhabitants like factotum, running businesses for the old guard, now invisible,
yet present in the diligence of dutiful workers.

You can take a taxi ride to the outskirts of the city,
the sprawling townships of Katatura,
where tourists revel through the night in make-shift taverns,
gaudy gigs contrived for those possessing dollars and pounds
to gawk at poverty in grotesque squalor.

Ah, Namibia! Like your sister in the south,
you settled to join a tarnished retinue of Africa's children
battling to be freed from the ownership of colonial masters.

Manger

The manger's empty, the child has vanished,
abducted by high priests of mercantilism and usury;
ransacked.

They say he's being kept in solitary confinement
to be released at a suitable hour
when whatever he says won't matter
since the turf's in the firm grip of tricksters.

The swaddling clothes are missing, too;
perhaps pawned or sold to the highest bidder
at a flea market for a few pieces of silver,
a joyless song.

In its place lies a serpent basking in scorching sun;
threatening to devour, its fangs hiss at wary seekers.

His mother, too, has left.
She's held captive in a cell with shadows.
No one can touch her, see her visage
or question the nature of her lament.
And the old carpenter, loyal companion,
disappeared quietly – did he abscond?

Dead, dry and obsolete,
myrrh and incense lie strewn on the arid ground.
All that's left of the event are some vague scribblings
about one star, a crib, lowly animals in a barn;
an embattled pantomime about conflict and betrayal.

Intermittently, few sift through details of the old story,
perhaps find new birth, a temple,
so as to live forever more,
and praise in between buying and selling.

28.

Remembering is to speak

Speaking to memories
revives and makes time seem foolish,
toothless

Speaking to quiet love
stirs and enlivens
within gentle hearts

Love songs
rise from old lyrical streets
in another country

Is remembering

Caricatures

They said: *drawings have never killed anyone,*
the subject's not sacred to us,
we live under OUR laws not THEIRS,
we will die to protect and defend the art of satire.

Then the crowd gathered round their bodies;
purpled rivulets saturating the floor of the office,
machines whirring during a dull, wintry mid-afternoon
as bodies, lifeless and limp, gave birth
to another spiral of hatred and fury; dead, wingless birds,
magnificent myths of free expression;
the drawings still stuck on a notice-board in a strange place;
a living sordid memory engulfed by passions
aroused by a different kind of sanctity,
smouldering there, waiting to ignite into flames,
devouring the artists, collaborations.

Someone would wag a finger and vow:
the drawings were never even funny
(the braver the bird, the fatter the cat),
that art does not survive in neutrality,
nothing is a stranger to ideology.

So worlds collide violently,
moving closer to their own truth
and dread.

KFC, Swakopmund

In the business zones, we walk, side by side,
with the offspring of our oppressors.
Sometimes their feeble mothers and fathers hobble along
and we help them to cross busy streets.

We serve them politely in franchises that they own:
Macdonalds, KFC, Nando's.
We are grateful – they give us jobs
so we can earn a living, feed our children.

We only wish that when they order at the counter,
they would look into our eyes,
not just mumble their hungry desires
under their breath.

Why do they avoid looking into our eyes?
Do they fear that they may see a yearning, a pain, reflected there?
Are they afraid they may just allow themselves, momentarily,
to see a person behind the servitude?

As it is, they slink out into their shiny cars and speed off
to the safe suburbs close to a cold, roaring Atlantic, Haka hana!*
As the sun sets we scramble for our taxis, ride to our shanties of shame
while they relax in air-conditioned, solid homesteads built on our foundations.

Haka hana - hurriedly – Herero expression

Desuetude

It lies in a corner,
war-torn shoes covered in dust,
tarnished, broken,
sometimes resembling shrapnel.

Nothing can restore or stir it though,
make it more visible.

Intermittently there's a discernible sediment
of hurt, anger even sorrow,
but not enough to resuscitate, mobilize,
re-surface again.

It's a cracked soul, pieces dispersed,
too brittle to assemble.

Just no sound purpose's left any longer to recount those histories, receded,
perhaps not entirely sanitised.

Remembering seems so redundant.
Like archiving oppression in comfortable libraries
for intellectuals to dissect,
the progeny of imperialists to theorise.

Eloquently useless.

In your hands

The gulls are all gone,
the sea is quiet. But the light in your eyes
illuminates the day like tiny stars;
soft clouds travel across the blue dome.

In this hour age is obscured into a shallow death;
richness rests in the lyrics of songsters whose music
eclipsed the tirades of tyrants,
tricksters robbing many of their time.

Left like great pretenders to mimic anthems,
the hollow in the soul filled with silent dreams
in lonely rooms on icy shores; bleak days;
a multitude of strangers whispered in half-baked tongues.

Sitting by my side, on this beach, in the changing season,
your arm around my waist as eras touch;
your warm, fresh breath blows the future across my sleeve,
all the demarcations of loss and sorrow dissipate.

Soon two continents, miles apart,
will be clasped firmly in your hands.

33.

Time, visages

So many endeared faces faded between hours;
a loss that's preserved in mottled memorials of joy.

These rest too in light captured in yesterday's
forever-young roaming through hearts' chambers.

The tyranny of time tempers desire, blood settles, cold.

Now wrapped in loose skin, bones and souls are penitent,
the pulse of passion's subdued, so's the fervour of youth's caress.

Innocence has loved and lost; a reassuring peck on the cheek
brushes away like a feather; querulous burdens cleaving age.

The new crusaders

The crusaders of literalism are alive and living in our midst
desecrating sacred images and vestiges of the Divine
ostensibly to safeguard and curb the threat of idolatry.

But unyielding obeisance to their crusades to stamp out a propensity
is merely substituting their own
controlling and thwarting spirituality.

Fences

In this neighbourhood, children grow up
faceless behind fences.

You measure their growth by listening
to their voices, changing gradually,

since you don't actually see them
just hear them giggling, splashing in the pool.

Later they guffaw with friends,
exuberant, and the music changes.

Then one day a baby cries and you guess
one of them's grown up, got married.

The father emerges one frosty morning through a gate
as you're watering the lawn.

You're surprised to see a silver-haired gentleman,
grumpy-looking.

A hand you've seen tossing your branches that grew over his fence
into your yard acquires a body

(his indignation always seemed
illustrated in the disorderliness of the pile).

The smell of pot-roasts has disappeared on Sundays;
no sound, only the constant whining of a lonely dog at night.

Indeed, changes occur behind fences in suburbs;
pity these walls deprive us of witness.

36.

While we were praying

I lost my favourite, old shoes in a mosque today.
I felt bewildered, quite unsafe,
even when the imam tried to console me, saying,
"There's a dua you must recite when you lose something.
It goes like this, *Inna lillahi.*"
I said: 'I know it' and repeated after him.

The prayer consoled for a while.
I tried to tell myself, "Well, someone else
in the world needed them more than I did.
They were old shoes, anyway."
Then I heard a man musing: 'It happens all the time.'
But, though commonplace,
something irreconcilable lingered.

Perhaps I wouldn't have felt the loss so seriously
when someone gave me an old pair of sandals
to go home with (a supreme act of kindness).
If only my shoes were not stolen
while I was praying ...
But then I remembered how a Palestinian
was gunned down by Israelis in Gaza
while the congregation was supplicating.
And no one could offer him anything.

Accord

Just when you think the ground's solid,
fissures crack in its surface after a storm;
treading becomes tricky.

A benign stranger enters quietly to fill crevices,
mend the path on your stride so reaching
that elusive post is easier.

But the path's worn by so many,
it's long, weather-beaten, and the burden on shoulders
is heavy, elicits pain.

In need of constant repair and care,
for many travellers it is a staff to lean on,
a companion to renew and inspire love.

Times change, discord between heads and hearts
demands a new verse, a song harmonious,
while the goal still shines.

Accord's not easy to find, souls easily bought
and sold like cattle make death imminent, inevitable:
so draws closer that vision sublime.

Interregnum

There are many citizens jumping off the ship like frightened rats.
They're rushing into rooms where the 'us' is blurred and the 'I' rules.
It's supremely ironic since they've lived in boxes for decades.
One would have believed there would be greater resilience,
more determination, tenacity to defer isolation.

No one said that it would be easy.
It never was, never will be, especially in settlements
where high prices are exchanged for low returns.
The time's never right for indulgent platitudes.
That's just a bad habit.

The money moguls are still signing off global clauses,
writing treaties to define the new dispensation,
while the poor and their children, wretched with large vacant eyes,
swarm the streets of cities, erecting shacks
in the vineyards of old landlords.

The statues of the old guard are being demolished, replaced with the new.
Nobody ever mentioned that before a harvest, there are many casualties.

Wreckage

A querulous pessimist said in the midst of the euphoria
that reigned during the season of change:
There's something about this arrangement
that warns we will soon have to scratch around
to find ourselves amid the wreckage.

Illusions can stifle awareness
of imminent danger and suffering.
What mattered then was that interlude of freedom
and a distant future shaped by possibility.

The festivals continued unabated & the abandonment
at the time was sufficient to nurture a dream.
But mirages betray notoriously,
a line diminishes between the real and the imagined.

Later, with feet on a stony surface,
the landscape's arid and thorny.
In the distance lies carnage of hopes
as smoke of burning buildings
contaminates an azure sky.

The image of a grey-haired warrior,
lost and forlorn, appears on the horizon.
Audible now, too, are his children's songs
of vengeance. In their eyes burn anger,
dread and the demise of decorum.

Fire. below

Again,the season of forced removals,
the beginning of the end, or the end
of another cycle, perhaps.

You know something's being replaced or removed
which should have disappeared ages ago.
It wasn't done before because somewhere
someone said the time wasn't right –
always the anthem of the well-heeled.

It was an enigmatic era of optimism
flowing from supposition,
a paradox which no one could duly decipher.
Maybe it was forgotten by the euphoria
or the romance of a silent revolution.

Suppose we do this, then that will happen
or maybe nothing will occur at all.
Sheer splendour of wallowing in speculation,
historical referencing.

But now anger can no longer be placated,
hunger and winter do not appease discontent.
There is no peace without justice
someone had shouted emphatically;
at that time no one bothered
to listen attentively.

The season of burning shacks has returned,
icons of the masters are being smeared with excrement,
tyres burn round the necks of marble statues.
All gasp at harvesting such crudity.

In dormitories, dissecting the fervent moment,
the discourses of learned scholars are being digitalized;
erudite articulations spar in coteries of the intelligentsia.
Nothing closes the rift between observers and those in the swell.

Down below, the duskland's ablaze;
the poor, whose burning hovels ignite the dark, grey skies,
are steadfast, diligently unpatriotic.

41.

Spectre

There's a dark shadow hovering on the edge of our lives.
It fails to be eclipsed by the indefatigable sunshine and never fades.
It's a stubborn spectre, intransigent phantom which clings,
refuses to vanish.

Usurping small victories, brave efforts to memorialize bitterness,
it makes its presence felt just when you believe compromise is possible.
Then it rears, thrusting its power with deadly weapons –
pangas, litanies of scorn and contempt.

Fuelled by fork-tongued monarchs with tin crowns on toppling thrones,
make-shift fiefdoms designed by scurrilous architects,
the war's called by countless names except 'scrambling for crumbs
left on tables after banquets of the ancient regime'.

So hopes of filial loyalty's consistently flushed
as Africa's dispossessed shuttle across broken borders,
driven to bare lands, hopeless, hungry, returning to betrayals,
empty promises of ancient patriarchs.

Ascension

is love:
to lay life on the altar, declare:
Death does not matter.
The burden of the cross erases borders.

It's abandoning the lure of being,
seduction by the delicacy of a rose,
witnessing sunrays glisten across a quiet ocean.
Placating inexorable desire:

a new kind of loving.
Traversing seven realms of sky and cosmic stars
on a winged white horse,
sublime with the breath of paradise.

Ascension's not easy loving.
It is a freedom that tastes of pain,
strife between living and dying.
But the victory of Love is immutable.

Separation

Death's at the door again, odourless, solemn and aloof.
Perhaps a few signs are scattered before arrival.
Jealous about triumph, the unexpected guest
usually interrupts the flow of simple routines.

When departing it usurps calm promises
concealed in a clear, blue sky;
colours of the world jettisoned into an abyss
with each visitation.

Just a hint of chiding pervades,
maybe about illusions of forever.
Sojourns, too, quite indiscriminately,
then vanishes with the kernel,
ruefully casting husks in the way as stark dials
for the ritual of separation.

Departure

There's a voice that speaks in the middle of the night, saying:
This is it. Be at peace, the slow circle of life's closing;
shut your eyes, sleep well; listen to the gentle rustling
of the leaves outside the window; it brings in its vibration,
a feeling that all is well, each path taken leading to rest.

What needs to be done is to release only what's necessary;
and to do that as silently, unobtrusively, as possible,
with a breath.

No additives needed. The value's within.
Nothing else really matters.
Fears or anguish have gone;
love's not weighed or measured anymore
but omnipresent.

Just a casual shrugging off of unsolved riddles;
mysteries linger somewhere – maybe nowhere?
Even pain and hunger have vanished.
All that remains now is to depart,
quietly.

Abu Bakr Solomons is a retired teacher-principal who has worked in primary and high schools in the townships of Cape Town for 40 years. He was the Chairperson of the Congress of South African Writers in 1990-1991. He was awarded a fellowship to pursue research in African literature at Northwestern University in Chicago in 1992. In 1993 he was invited to participate in the Salzburg Seminar in Austria. His work has been published in COSAW journals, a Botsotso publication and two Sol Plaatje-European Union anthologies.

Printed in the United States
by Baker & Taylor Publisher Services